SandCastle
United We Stand

Patriotism

Pam Scheunemann

Consulting Editor
Monica Marx, M.A./Reading Specialist

ABDO Publishing Company

Published by SandCastle™, an imprint of ABDO Publishing Company, 4940 Viking Drive, Edina, Minnesota 55435.

Printed in the United States.

Credits
Edited by: Pam Price
Curriculum Coordinator: Nancy Tuminelly
Cover and Interior Design and Production: Mighty Media
Photo Credits: Corbis Images, Comstock, PhotoDisc

Library of Congress Cataloging-in-Publication Data
Scheunemann, Pam, 1955-
    Patriotism / Pam Scheunemann.
        p. cm. -- (United we stand)
    Includes index.
    Summary: Defines patriotism as being proud of your country and provides examples and symbols such as the flying of the flag, saying the Pledge of Allegiance, and voting.
    ISBN 1-57765-880-9
    1. Patriotism--United States--Juvenile literature. [1. Patriotism.] I. Title. II. Series.

JK1759 .S34 2002
323.6'5'0973--dc21

                                                              2002025445

SandCastle™ books are created by a professional team of educators, reading specialists, and content developers around five essential components that include phonemic awareness, phonics, vocabulary, text comprehension, and fluency. All books are written, reviewed, and leveled for guided reading, early intervention reading, and Accelerated Reader® programs and designed for use in shared, guided, and independent reading and writing activities to support a balanced approach to literacy instruction.

Let Us Know

After reading the book, SandCastle would like you to tell us your stories about reading. What is your favorite page? Was there something hard that you needed help with? Share the ups and downs of learning to read. We want to hear from you! To get posted on the ABDO Publishing Company Web site, send us email at:

sandcastle@abdopub.com

SandCastle Level: Transitional

What is patriotism?

3

Patriotism means being proud of your country.

There are many ways to show your patriotism.

Each country has its own flag.

People fly the flags of their own country to show their patriotism.

They are proud of their country.

We show our patriotism when we fly the American flag.

It is an important symbol of our country.

My grandpa shows his patriotism by hanging the flag outside his home.

He is proud to be an American.

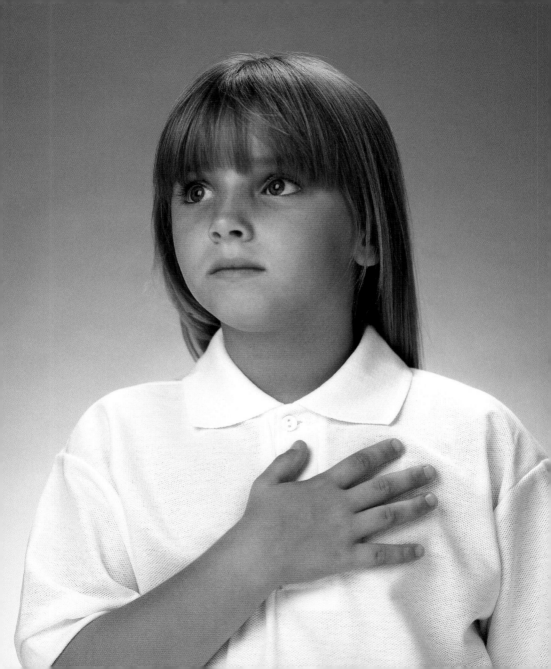

We show our patriotism by saying the Pledge of Allegiance.

We are proud to be Americans.

We show our patriotism by singing "The Star Spangled Banner."

The song is about our flag.

We sing it to show we are proud of our country.

We can show our
patriotism by wearing
red, white, and blue.

These are the colors
in the flag.

Red stands for courage,
white stands for truth,
and blue stands for justice.

We can show our patriotism by supporting our soldiers.

They help to protect America and keep it a free country.

They are proud to be Americans.

We have special days to celebrate our patriotism.

Which one falls on July 4th?

(Independence Day)

Index

Glossary

allegiance   to be loyal to someone or something

American   a citizen of the United States of America

patriotism   love and devotion to one's country

pledge   a promise or agreement

proud   to have satisfaction in and respect for someone or something you or others have done

symbol   an object used to represent something

About SandCastle™

A professional team of educators, reading specialists, and content developers created the SandCastle™ series to support young readers as they develop reading skills and strategies and increase their general knowledge. The SandCastle™ series has four levels that correspond to early literacy development in young children. The levels are provided to help teachers and parents select the appropriate books for young readers.

Emerging Readers
(no flags)

Beginning Readers
(1 flag)

Transitional Readers
(2 flags)

Fluent Readers
(3 flags)

These levels are meant only as a guide. All levels are subject to change.

To see a complete list of SandCastle™ books and other nonfiction titles from ABDO Publishing Company, visit www.abdopub.com or contact us at:
4940 Viking Drive, Edina, Minnesota 55435 • 1-800-800-1312 • fax: 1-952-831-1632